The Top Ten Mistakes Leaders Make

A Listening Guide & Workbook

By Hans Finzel

Adapted from "The Top Ten Mistakes Leaders Make"
by Hans Finzel, Published by David C Cook
2007, Colorado Springs, CO

© 2017 Top Ten Enterprises
9457 S University #712
Highlands Ranch, CO 80126-4976

Hans Finzel

Dr. Hans Finzel is a successful author, speaker and trusted authority in the field of leadership. For 20 years he served as President of international non-profit WorldVenture, working in over 65 countries. Hans speaks, writes and teaches on practical leadership principles from the real world—not just the classroom.

He has written ten books, including his bestseller, "The Top Ten Mistakes Leaders Make" (David C Cook). Hans has trained leaders on five continents and his books have been translated into over twenty foreign languages. Today he serves as President of HDLeaders and teaches and speaks globally on all things leadership. Hans and his wife Donna have four grown children and make their home in Colorado.

Contact Hans at hansfinzel.com
Twitter: hansfinzel
Facebook: facebook.com/hansfinzel
YouTube: youtube.com/hansfinzel

To Benefit from
"The Top Ten Mistakes Leaders Make" Listening Guide

- Introduce yourself to Hans Finzel
- Mute your cell phone please
- Participate with other attendees in discussions and answering questions
- Take notes and fill in the blanks in this workbook
- Look for major "Aha moments" and highlight those in your notes
- Be sure and stop by the book table and grab some other great leadership resources
- Take time to discuss your takeaways with your team over a meal in the next week

What Others Say
About Top Ten Mistakes Leaders Make

Most leadership books have a short shelf life, but Hans' book has endured the test of time. It's a great read on servant leadership.

Rick Warren, pastor, Saddleback Church; author, The Purpose Driven Life

This is one of the most practical books on leadership I have in my own personal library. If you are serious about becoming a better leader, you will want to read this book.

John C. Maxwell, author, speaker, and founder, The INJOY Group, Atlanta, Georgia

Thank you, Hans, for not just giving us 'servant-leadership' language, but for showing us how to be servant-leaders. And you have done it in a wonderfully appealing way. As we avoid the ten 'minefields' you outlined, we will become leaders of integrity and authenticity."

Crawford W. Loritts Jr., author, radio host, speaker, and pastor, Fellowship Bible Church, Roswell, Georgia

"Hans Finzels' book is a 'truth in the trenches' approach to leadership.
Having identified the core causes of leadership failure, his counsel for correction will remind you of the consummate leader we have in Jesus Christ. This is one of the best books I have read on the subject of leadership ... I recommend it highly!"

Mark L. Bailey, President, Dallas Theological Seminary

The Top Ten Mistakes Leaders Make
A Listening Guide and Workbook

Table of Contents

The Top Ten Mistakes Leaders Make

An Introduction to Leaders and Leadership

Definition: "Leadership is *influence*."
- Anyone who influences someone else to do something has led that person.
- *A leader takes people where they would never go on their own.*"

Leadership Observations: Four observations about leadership in general

1. If you do what comes natural _____

2. People are confused _____

3. There seem to be more _____

4. Churches and ministries need _____

> "We spend a lot of time teaching leaders what to do. We don't spend enough time teaching leaders what to stop. Half the leaders I have met don't need to learn what to do. They need to learn what to stop."
> - Peter Drucker

Leadership can be dangerous. We hold the power to do irreparable damage to our followers by the mistakes we make. People ask me, "Hans, have you made all these mistakes?" "Are you kidding," I answer. "I have made hundreds. I only included the top ten most dangerous ones." The greatest lessons I've learned about good leadership have been through my own mistakes. (pages 14,16)

Chapter One
The Top-Down Attitude

This is the mother of all leadership hang-ups. It is foundational to all the rest of the mistakes. "If you have it, you will spread it to everything your leadership hands touch." (page 25)

The top-down attitude is defined by people who believe that everyone should serve them, as opposed to believing they should be serving others within the institution. (page 32)

What is the Top Down Attitude?

* I'm on top because _____

* I'm the boss so _____

* I'm the leader so I am going _____

* I make all the _____

Six results of having the top-down attitude

1. Abusive _____

2. Dictatorship _____

3. Dirty _____

4. Lack of _____

5. Controlling _____

6. Egocentric _____

What is the alternative to top-down leadership?

_____ Leadership

Two most important passages in the New Testament on servant leadership:

- John 13:1-17
- Philippians 2:1-4

Servant Leadership: *When the leader cares more about the good of the team than his or her own enrichment.*

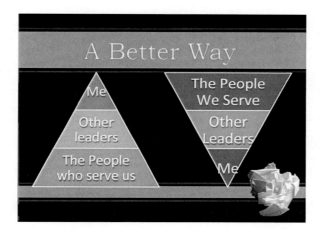

What is the difference between servant leadership and slave leadership? What is servant leadership not?

_____

_____

_____

_____

_____

_____

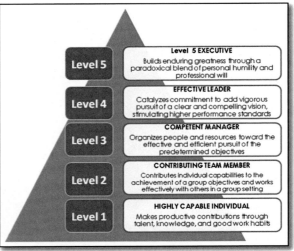

Six Takeaways

- *Not Abusive Authority*: But _____

- *Not Dictatorship*: But _____ in the process

- *Not Deplorable Delegation*: But give them _____to do their job

- *Not Lack of Listening:* But exercising a _____

- *Not Controlling*: But _____

- Not Egocentric: But the _____ of others

Questions for discussion

1. How would you describe the problem of top down leadership?

2. Do you agree that it is a problem?

3. If not, why not?

4. If so, where have you seen it show up in your workplace?

Chapter Two
Putting Paperwork before Peoplework

Since this chapter was first written, we have had an explosion of technology. The social media revolution and the all-pervasive development of smart phones, has taken the issue of information over people to a whole new level. It's not only paperwork that distracts us, but all those bits and bytes that make it to our smart phones, tablets and laptops.   Leadership is still about people work. 90% of the leader's effectiveness continues to be his or her ability to work well with people and to really focus on people.

> **People are opportunities, not interruptions**

Here's a simple but reliable test to discover whether you are task- or people-oriented. When someone walks into your office...and interrupts your task at hand for the sake of conversation, how do you react? Do you view that person as an interruption or an opportunity? Does your face brighten as your people antenna powers up, or do you grimace inside at this 'interruption'? (page 45)

The three big problems of leadership and paperwork:

1. The greater the leadership role, _____

2. The greater the leadership role, _____

3. People must be seen as _____

We were not looking for praise from people, not from you or anyone else, even though as apostles of Christ we could have asserted our authority. Instead, we were like young children among you. Just as a nursing mother cares for her children, so we cared for you. Because we loved you so much, we were delighted to share with you not only the gospel of God but our lives as well. The Apostle Paul - 1 Thes, 2:6-8 NIV

A few years ago I met an old professor at the University of Notre Dame. Looking back on his long life of teaching, he said with a funny twinkle in his eyes: "I have always been complaining that my work was constantly interrupted, until I slowly discovered that my interruptions were my work." This is the great conversion in life: to recognize and believe that the many unexpected events are not just disturbing interruptions of our projects, but the way in which God molds our hearts and prepares us for his return.

- Henri J. Nouwen, Out of Solitude

You might be a paper pusher if …
What are some of the signs of putting paperwork/technology over peoplework?

- _____ Type "A"

- _____ personality

- People are seen as _____

- _____and _____ focused

- "I live by _____"

- I tend to _____ people

- I listen _____ - if at all

- I am Impatient - "_____!"

- Ruled by _____pressure

- Evaluate myself based on _____

A capacity for solitude is what nurtures great relationships. But in today's always-on social media world, our solitude has been replaced by incessant online updates, which both weaken our sense of self and our ability to create genuine friendships.

-Sherry Turkle; Director, MIT Initiative on Technology and Self

Leadership is Peoplework!

There are eleven suggestions that Dr. Finzel shares about how to push aside the paper and technology and make more room for people. Write them down here and circle the three that you want to be sure and practice.

1. Judge your success by _____

2. Love your _____

3. Love your _____

4. Plan team _____ and _____

5. Take your _____

6. Go to people's _____

7. See people as _____

8. Get out of your _____

9. Don't _____ others

10. Go on a _____ vacation

11. M_____ _____ _____ _____

Questions for discussion:

1. Where do you fit on the continuum of people oriented versus task oriented?

2. How do you feel when people interrupt you at work?

3. What are some best practices you use or could suggest to make room for people in your workplace?

4. What was the best suggestion that you got from this chapter?

Chapter Three
The Absence of Affirmation

Affirmation must be a part of every leader's toolkit. It is amazing how many times people overlook this simple but powerful piece of leadership.

People don't care how much you know until they know how much you care.

> And of all personal touches, I find the short, handwritten 'nice job' note to have the highest impact.
>
> - Tom Peters

What could be better than a pay raise?

1. Everyone thrives on _____

2. We wildly underestimate the power of _____

3. Learn to read the varying levels of _____

> **Compliments Dissolve Quickly**
>
> One of the commodities in life that most people can't get enough of is a compliment. The ego is never so intact that one can't find a hole in which to plug a little praise. But, compliments by their very nature are highly biodegradable and tend to dissolve hours or days after we receive them—which is why we can always use another.
>
> —Phyllis Theroux

Why Don't Some Leaders Affirm?

Why do you suppose that some leaders never affirm or praise their followers?

- Family _____

- Never _____

- Fear of _____

- _____

- Never learned _____

Learn to recognize where your key team players are on the following affirmation continuum:

Source: *Three Signs of a Miserable Job*, Patrick Lencioni (Jossy-Bass)

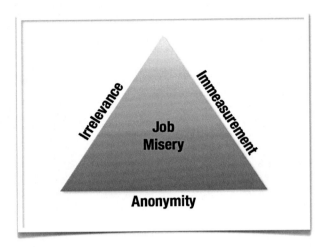

Four Takeaways

1. We leaders must _____!

2. Everyone thrives on _____ and _____

3. _____ and _____ have a short shelf life.

4. Learn to read the varying levels of _____

Questions for discussion:

1. On a scale of 1 to 10, 10 being the best, how do or would people rate you as a person who gives good affirmation?

2. Can you think of someone right now that could use your affirmation? Could you make a list of three?

3. Describe a recent case where you were affirmed, and share how that feedback gave you a huge boost.

4. What was a best idea you gained from this chapter?

Chapter Four
No Room for Mavericks

A huge mistake leaders make is to shut down mavericks. *Maverick* is another word for

- _____
- _____
- _____
- _____
- _____

They're often not as comfortable to work with, but they're absolutely essential for every organization. We tend to under appreciate Mavericks. We drive them away by our policies and procedures. We need to learn to look for and harness the creativity of truly useful Mavericks.

The term "Maverick" came from a man by the name of Samuel A. Maverick who died in1870. He was a Texas pioneer who did not brand his calves.   He thought is was not a great idea and chose to identify his cattle in other ways. He did not go along with the norms. Definition: "An independent individual who does not go along with a group or party."

> In times of change, learners inherit the earth, while the learned find themselves beautifully equipped, to deal with a world that no longer exists.
>
> - Eric Hoffer

Take a lesson from our US Military that has a hard time changing. "If you don't like change, you're going to like irrelevance even less." General Eric Shinseki, Former US Army Chief of Staff (4 Star General)

Mavericks are the very people that can stop our slide from...

> *Inspiration to institution*
> *Passion to paralysis*
> *Movement to monument*
> *Apostolic to mechanistic*
> *Bravado to bureaucracy*
> *Dynamic to dead*

Organizational Lifecycles

This diagram shows the normal life cycle of every organization and ministry.   Is it inevitable to slide down the far side?   What does it take for leaders to break the cycle down the dark side toward bureaucracy and death?

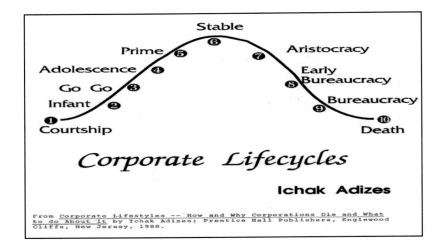

One of the best ways to take the wind out of the sails of visionaries is to send their ideas to a committee. Have we made it impossible for bright rising stars and maverick go-getters to live within our organization? When we become too preoccupied with policy, procedure, and the fine-tuning of conformity to organizational standards, in effect, we squeeze out some of our most gifted people. Mavericks are messy by nature.... Mavericks are necessary for us to be creative. Mavericks are free spirits that have always been misunderstood. (pages 74-75)

> If I'd have asked my customers what they wanted, they would have told me, 'a faster horse!'
> - Henry Ford
>
> Our job is to read things that are not yet on the page.
> - Steve Jobs

The Eleven Commandments of Organizational Paralysis

1. "That's _____."
2. "We _____ that way around here."
3. "We've _____done it that way."
4. "It's _____ a change for us."
5. "We tried something like that before and _____."
6. "I wish it were _____."
7. "It's against _____to do it that way."
8. "When you've _____, you'll understand."
9. "Who gave you _____ to change the rules?"
10. "_____, okay?"
11. "How dare you suggest that what _____!"

Aim for a flexible response to policies and procedures. If you're in senior management or on the board and in control, take some risk and bring some fresh young blood into the equation. Give them room to succeed. Rules are made to be broken, principles are not. (Page 84)

We Need to Cultivate Mavericks

1. _____ for them

2. _____ to them

3. _____from them

4. Give them a _____

5. Put them _____

My greatest fear is becoming _____

_____ is a bigger

risk than _____.

The Three Deadliest Phrases for a Maverick

1. We _____ and it didn't work
2. We've _____done it that way!
3. We've _____done it that way!

Questions for Discussion:

1. Define the term maverick as used in this chapter.

2. Would you consider yourself a maverick?

3. Do you work with any Mavericks that are misunderstood?

4. What's the best way to tell the difference between a maverick and a troublemaker?

Chapter Five
Dictatorship in Decision Making

Leadership is all about decision-making all. But how we make decisions as leaders is not easy. If we do what comes natural, we will probably make all the decisions ourselves. And we might think we should because we are the leader.

On the other hand, great leaders learn the fine art of decision-making that allows for input from the team. Yes, the buck stops with the leader, but that doesn't mean there's not a lot of room for dialogue and listening on the part of a leader.

> Fundamental values are not chosen from thin air based on the desires of executives, they are discovered within what already exists in an organization.
> —Jim Collins, Built to Last

Let's talk about organization charts. Do you have one? Is it clear? Has it been updated recently and does it actually reflect reality? Most traditional org charts help dictators dictate. They are at the top so they are given all the reason in the world to work "down" to all the others and act with command and control. There is no perfect org chart but I recommend you make one that shows the value of everyone on the team.

Today's young leaders especially love flat organizations and very much resist leaders hidden away in ivory towers sending down edicts from above.

How Dictators Operate

1. They _____ decisions.

2. They view truth _____

3. They _____ decisions _____

4. They love to _____

5. They are neither _____ or _____

How Consensus Leaders Operate

1. They _____ decisions

2. They _____

3. They view truth _____

4. They are _____

5. They see people _____

6. They give their people _____

7. They let those who are responsible

   _____

Truly A Better Way To Lead

To the elders among you, I appeal as a fellow elder and a witness of Christ's sufferings who also will share in the glory to be revealed: Be shepherds of God's flock that is under your care, watching over them—not because you must, but because you are willing, as God wants you to be; not pursuing dishonest gain, but eager to serve; not lording it over those entrusted to you, but being examples to the flock. And when the Chief Shepherd appears, you will receive the crown of glory that will never fade away.
In the same way, you who are younger, submit yourselves to your elders. All of you, clothe yourselves with humility toward one another, because,

"God opposes the proud but shows favor to the humble."

I Peter 5: 1-5 NIV

Questions for Discussion:

1. How would people rate you as a decision-maker?
2. On a scale of 1 to 10, 10 being consensus building and 1 being controlling, where would you fit?
3. Give an example of a time a decision was made poorly in your work environment and it caused you great frustration.
4. What's the best advice you received in this chapter on proper decision-making?

> Take away my people but leave my factories and soon grass will grow on the factory floor. Take away my factories but leave my people and soon we will have a new and better factory."
> —Andrew Carnegie

Chapter 6
Dirty Delegation

This chapter builds right on top of chapter 5. In fact it is first cousin to dictatorship. When people want to control all the decisions, they make lousy delegators. Decision-making and delegation go hand-in-hand. Many time people who are control freaks are very controlling in their decision-making, and therefore are terrible at good delegation practices.

> I don't have a problem with delegation. I love to delegate. I am either lazy enough, or busy enough, or trusting enough, or congenial enough, that the notion of leaving tasks in someone else's lap doesn't just sound wise to me, it sounds attractive.
> – John Ortberg

Great delegation is like great discipleship. We are actually developing the potential in others. Here are seven "wins" that occur when you learn to be a great delegator:

The Results of Great Delegation

- It _____people

- It _____ people

- It taps into the _____

- It builds a strong _____

- It spreads _____

- It empowers _____

- It's about _____ not _____

It seems that more gifted and talented you are, the harder it is to be a great delegator. You can do a lot of things better than other people! That is one problem. Also, it seems that some insecure personality types(control freaks) really find it very hard to release work to others.

Why It's Hard To Delegate Well

1. Fear of _____

2. Fear of _____

3. Fear of _____

4. Unwillingness to _____

5. Fear of _____

6. Lack of _____

7. Fear of losing _____

8. Fear of _____

Four Questions That Every Follower Asks

1. What do you _____

2. Will you let me _____

3. Will you _____

4. Will you _____

> The best executive is the one who has sense enough to pick good men(and women) to do what he wants done, and self-restraint enough to keep from meddling with them while they do it.
> -Theodore Roosevelt

> The five stages of great delegation
>
> 1. Assignment
> 2. Authority
> 3. Accountability
> 4. Affirmation
> 5. Availability

Jesus Had No "Plan B"

Jesus was history's greatest delegator. What task has ever been assigned to others with more impact than the fulfillment of the Great Commission? He poured three years into his twelve men and left them with history's greatest delegation. Notice that Jesus did a masterful job at following what we discern as the five steps of great accountability. And He had no back up plan if this plan failed.

Then Jesus came to them and said, "All authority in heaven and on earth has been given to me. Therefore go and make disciples of all nations, baptizing them in the name of the Father and of the Son and of the Holy Spirit, and teaching them to obey everything I have commanded you. And surely I am with you always, to the very end of the age." – Matthew 18:18-20

Questions for Discussion:

1. On a scale of 1 to 10, 10 being best, how would people rate you as a delegator?

2. What are the results of poor delegation in the workplace?

3. What do you think are one or two of the most important principles to be a good delegator?

4. What do you feel is most helpful to you in this chapter?

Chapter 7
Communication Chaos

Communication is the lifeblood of any organization. It's the job of leadership to communicate clearly and constantly. If people don't know what's going on, they think the worst. Lack of information is highly demotivating to workers.

Leaders must figure out ways to tap into that underground flow of information. They must keep current on the undercurrents. The more people you lead, the more you must listen. Effective leadership has more to do with listening than with talking. Listen to those who are in the trenches and rely on that information to make wise decisions. Nothing stops the progress of an organization more quickly than leaders failing to listen. Like hardening of the arteries clogs the flow of blood, too little communication will hurt a leader's credibility. (pages 138,140)

> The Void Created by the failure to communicate is soon filled with poison, drivel and misrepresentation.
> - C. Northcote Parkinson

Communication Chaos

- Never assume _____

- The bigger the group, _____

- When left in the dark, people tend to _____

- Communication must be the _____ of effective leader

> A corporation's values are its life's blood. Without effective communication, actively practiced, without the art of scrutiny, those values will disappear in a sea of trivial memos and impertinent reports. There may be no single thing more important in our efforts to achieve meaningful work and fulfilling relationships than to learn and practice the art of communication.
> —Max De Pree, *Leadership Is an Art*

Communication in the Lifecycles of Organizations

As you look over this diagram, where would you say you are in your organization? Do you think it is time to move more toward the right? What signs do you see that things are not as good as they could be?

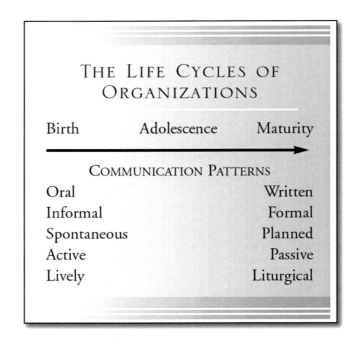

Why Don't Leaders Communicate Enough?

Most leaders don't communicate enough. It is amazing how many leaders think that the troops know what is going on when in reality, they really are totally in the dark. Sometimes the leader thinks that the communication happens magically through osmosis. Other times they think that they communicated to all when they really communicated with just a few. (Only the inner circle is informed)

Why don't some leaders communicate?

1. Too little _____

2. Too many _____

3. _____

4. _____

5. Too much _____

6. _____

7. Communication _____

> Certainly a leader needs a clear vision of the organization and where it is going, but a vision is of little value unless it is shared in a way so as to generate enthusiasm and commitment. Leadership and communication are inseparable.
> - Claude I. Taylor Chairman of the Board, Air Canada

Questions for Discussion:

1. On a scale of 1 to 10, 10 being the best, how would you rate the general flow of communication in your workplace?

2. If you scored six or below, give some examples of how communication could be improved.

3. What would you like to hear from the people above you on a regular basis?

4. What is one of the best things you learned from this chapter?

Chapter 8
Missing the Clues of Corporate Culture

Every group has its own unique culture. Whether you are a church, a business, a fire station, a school or a Fortune 500 company, you have a culture that is unique to you. Culture is simply "the way we do things around here."   Families have cultures and every group that works together has a distinct culture. We can understand our workplace better when we understand the culture.

The Danger of Missing Corporate Culture Clues

- Corporate culture is _____

- Never underestimate the _____

- _____ should be one of leadership's top priorities

- Learn to respect _____

Corporate Value Statements

- Like _____: They help leaders hold an organization together.
- Like _____: They attract newcomers as members, employees, customers, or donors.
- Like _____: By which a leader can measure how his or her group is doing

WILLOW CREEK
COMMUNITY CHURCH

The Vision of Willow Creek Church

Turn irreligious people into fully devoted followers of Jesus Christ

The Seven Values of Trader Joe's

1. Integrity
2. We are a product driven company
3. At Trader Joe's we create WOW customer experience every day
4. No Bureaucracy
5. We are a national chain of neighborhood grocery stores
6. Kaizen (continuous improvement)
7. The store is our brand

The Value of Understanding Your Organization's Culture

1.   Fosters strong feelings of _____

2.   Promotes high levels of _____

3.   Facilitates consensus about _____

4.   Encourages _____

5.   Reduces levels of _____ and _____

6.   Promotes strong norms about _____ and _____

Source of this list of six: Kouzes and Posner, *The Leadership Challenge*

> When you walk into a new organization for the first time, you can feel the culture much more than an insider can. (page 155)

Six Reactions to Culture Conflict (page 173)

Conformer
"I've just got to _____."

Complainer
"I may have to work here, but _____."

Innovator
"Let's _____!"

Ritualist
"Job? What job? I'm just _____."

Retreatist
"I've got to _____!"

Rebel
"They can't make me _____—I'll show them!"

Questions for Discussion:
1. What are some positive distinguishing characteristics of the culture where you work?

2. Building on the first question, what are some negative characteristics of your culture?

3. Why do people like working where you work? Or do they?

4. Why do people do not enjoy working in your workplace? What frustrates them that's part of your culture?

Chapter 9
Success without Successors is Failure

No one is indispensable. That's right, I am talking to you. Sooner or later we will have to move on. One of the last great acts of leadership in any role is to prepare others to take your place. The idea of finding our replacements should not be a threat, but the final fulfillment of great leadership.   Great leaders surround themselves with a cast of great characters who can follow them.

Make a Mark – Leave A Legacy

What is more important to you in the long run, making a mark or leaving a legacy? Actually great leaders do both as they finish well and leave well. To end well, we must not get too wrapped up in our own indispensability. Humility is the key to finishing well and passing the torch on to our successors. One of the keys to a successful leadership transition is to learn to hold our positions loosely. (page 191)

> Leaders tend to stay too long in a position rather than leave too soon.
>
> Leaders do more damage by staying too long than by leaving too soon.
>
> - Lyle Schaller

Barriers to Successful Successions

There are as many unsuccessful leadership transitions as there are successful ones.   These are some of the many reasons why leaders don't do well following other leaders. (page 183)

- The organization doesn't like the new person.
- The new person doesn't like the organization.
- The new person's family can't adjust to the new city they moved to.
- There is a corporate culture conflict: Values and beliefs don't match.
- The leader fails miserably in his newly assigned responsibilities. He or she lacks

the ability, capacity, experience, or knowledge to do the job well.
- The old guard sabotages the efforts of the new leader.
- The old leader sabotages the efforts of the new leader.
- The old leader fails to leave, or reappears.
- The new leader lacks persistence in implementing changes.
- The new leader is recruited away by a better offer or challenge.
- The new leader fails to win a following because of poor interpersonal skills.

Can you think of some other reasons that I have not mentioned?

_____

Why Is It That Some Leaders Can't Let Go When It Is Time?

1. Fear of _____

2. Resistance to _____

3. Self _____

4. Lack of confidence _____

5. Love for _____ and the _____

6. Loss of _____

> To finish well end well, we must not get too wrapped up in our own indispensability. Humility is the key to finishing well and passing the torch on to our successors. One of the keys to a successful leadership transition is to learn to hold our positions loosely. (page 191)

A leader needs all different kinds of mentoring relationships to succeed in his or her leadership. Mentoring includes upward (someone more advanced mentoring you), downward (you mentoring those below you), internal peer (peers inside your organization) and external peer (peers outside your organization). (page 188)

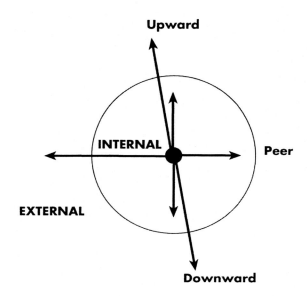

Three great examples from the Bible of finishing well as the big leader had the humility to mentor their replacements:

- Moses developed Joshua to take the reins (Deut. 34)
- Jesus trained his twelve (John 20:21)
- Paul taught Timothy everything he knew to carry on the work (II Timothy 2)

Questions for Discussion:
1. If you were run over by a bus tomorrow morning, is there anybody on your team who could replace you?
2. Name two people that you are mentoring right now.
3. If you're the top leader, is there a succession plan in place?
4. What was the most helpful principle for you in this chapter?

Chapter 10
Failure to Focus on the Future

The future is rushing toward us at breakneck speed. If there's one thing that is constant it is change. Leaders are paid to think about the future and to anticipate what lies around the next corner. It could be the greatest opportunity ever to come along, or a giant roadblock that will take us out. This final chapter rightly talks about the leader's role in planning ahead for the organization, business, church or school.

Leaders are paid to be dreamers. In fact, the higher you go in leadership, the more your work is about the future. I have very little influence on what is going to happen in my organization in the next six months, but I am making daily decisions that could have a profound impact on us five years down the road. (page 208)

> Leaders are pioneers. They are people who venture into unexplored territory. They guide us to new and often unfamiliar destinations. People who take the lead are the foot soldiers in the campaigns for change. The unique reason for having leaders— their differentiating function—is to move us forward. Leaders get us going someplace.
> —Kouzes and Posner, The Leadership Challenge

"Where there is no vision, the people perish.
But he that keeps the law, happy is he."
— Proverbs 29:18

Why is Vision so Essential in Leadership?
As you look over this list, circle any of these issues plaguing your group

- Improve results
- Inspire the troops
- Attract people to our cause
- Move us forward
- Grow our ministry

- Reach our goals

- Repair damage

- Build new momentum

- Cast new hope

- Raise the bar

- Get people off their seats

- Kingdom fruit!

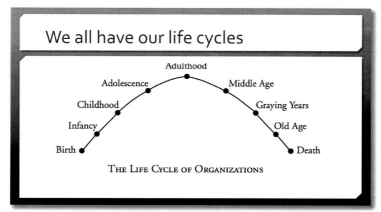

There is no more powerful engine driving an organization toward excellence and long-range success than an attractive, worthwhile, achievable vision for the future, widely shared.

- Burt Nanus, Visionary Leadership

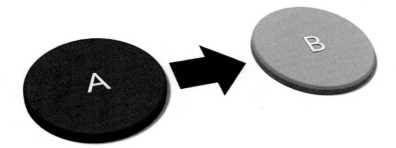

Leaders take people to places they would never go themselves. Vision is where the leaders are taking their people from point "A" to point "B." That is what vision is all about. Moses had a call to take the Israelites from point A – Egypt to point B, the Promised Land. In his case the vision was clear—it was geographical. In our case, sometimes the greatest challenge of the leadership team is to agree on the "B."

Two Great Definitions of Vision

Vision is a picture of the future that produces passion in people.

- Bill Hybels

Vision is a clear picture of what could be, fueled by the conviction that it should be.

- Andy Stanley

Questions for Discussion:

1. How future savvy are you? Do you think a lot about the future or do you like to live in the present? Or is it more of the past that you like to think about?

2. In thinking about the future for your organization, what are some big trends that you see on the horizon? Which of them are opportunities? How about threats?

3. Would you say you are more worried or more confident about the future of your group/organization? Why?

4. What is your favorite quote in this chapter?

Your Aha Moments

I have left this page intentionally blank so that you can write down some of the biggest "ah ha" moments from the presentation. What hit you the hardest? What did you find most useful? What are some of your most memorable takeaways?

Other Books by Hans Finzel

The Top Ten Ways to Be A Great Leader
David C Cook   (Print and Kindle)

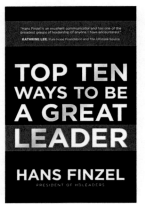

After 30 years in the trenches of leadership, I decided to asked the question, "What are the most important skills every new leader should master?" I came up with an acrostic for the word LEADERSHIP. Each chapter of this book, 10 chapters in all, outlines an essential skill every leader must master. The "Top 10 Mistakes Leaders Make" is about pitfalls to avoid. This book is about essential skills every leader needs to be successful.

1. "L" Is for Listen and Learn
2. "E" Is for Emotional Intelligence
3. "A" Is for Accessibility
4. "D" Is for Determination
5. "E" Is for Effective Communication
6. "R" Is for Resilience
7. "S" Is for Servant Attitude
8. "H" Is for Hands Off Delegation
9. "I" Is for Integrity
10. "P" Is for the Power of Humility

The Power of Passion in Leadership
Top Ten Enterprises (Audio, Print and Kindle)

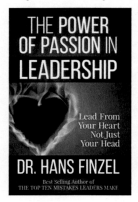

In this brand new book you will learn what it means to work in your "passion zone." Hans explains from his own career journey, how to find your passion zone and what action steps to take if you are far from that place of fulfillment. People love following leaders whose hearts are fueled by passion. This book will help you uncover what passion in your work really is, and how to find it, no matter what stage you are at in your career. The advice in this book is especially powerful for anyone in a role of leadership that is experiencing **boredom** or **burn out**. Life is too short to settle for less than the best—especially if we are called to lead other people.

Top Ten Leadership Commandments
David C Cook (Print and Kindle)

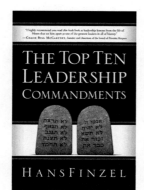

This leadership classic is based on the life and legacy of Moses. Hans says, "I happen to think he is one of the greatest leaders in history because he had such a tough leadership assignment but did not quit!"

The life of Moses provides a master study on what it means to be an effective leader. Consider his pedigree: Answered the call to do something beyond his means; stood his ground before kings; led millions of people on a journey across rivers and through deserts. Moses did this all with a dogged persistence that would not give up. You will discover a dynamic, effective tool for developing leadership skills, all built on the solid foundation of God's word.

Change is Like a Slinky
Moody Press Northfield (Print and Kindle)

This is a practical guide to navigate change in today's organizational climate. Change or perish: this is a current motto for leaders in all types of organizations.

But how does one adapt to such fast and furious change and effectively lead the organization through change?

Hans provides a proven strategy in Change is Like a Slinky, exploring the six major phases in the cycle of change. As he says, "Change is a lot like a Slinky... A slinky can be a lot of fun, but it is also completely unpredictable."

Instead of grudgingly wading through inevitable change, readers will find themselves equipped and fired up to tackle it head on.

Launch Your Encore
Baker Books (Print and Kindle)

No longer retiring at 65 and dying soon there after, people are ending up with a whole lot of life left after their main careers are over. A lot of boomers are asking the post career question, "What's next?" Most of us don't believe in the "R" word, traditional retirement. Launch Your Encore is the answer to the "what's next," question. We explore how to find adventure and purpose later in life with intentionality. There are dangers to avoid and adventures to explore. Our passion is to help you find meaning and purpose in your sixties, seventies, and eighties (What we have coined as the 60-80 window). With the average U.S. life expectancy reaching eighty, we are entering an exciting new life stage. It just might be that our final act is our greatest.

Unlocking The Scriptures
David C Cook (Print and Kindle)

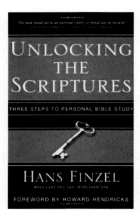

Even though there are many resources on Bible study methods, I fully recommend this book for the serious Bible student. This is a classic book on inductive Bible study.

This updated classic leads the reader through the inductive Bible study process, showing practically how to dig into serious Bible study on your own.

With this tool, Christians can learn to relevantly apply God's Word to their lives as His Spirit leads them personally, rather than as some other leader might direct. Unlocking the Scriptures provides practical examples that walk the reader through the steps of unpacking Scripture, using actual passages to practice. Free downloadable study guide and activities.

47350011R00024

Made in the USA
San Bernardino, CA
31 March 2017